Happiness

HBR Emotional Intelligence Series

How to be human at work

The HBR Emotional Intelligence Series features smart, essential reading on the human side of professional life from the pages of *Harvard Business Review*.

Empathy

Happiness

Mindfulness

Resilience

Other books on emotional intelligence from *Harvard Business Review*:

HBR's 10 Must Reads on Emotional Intelligence

HBR Guide to Emotional Intelligence

Happiness

HBR EMOTIONAL INTELLIGENCE SERIES

Harvard Business Review Press

Boston, Massachusetts

Library of Congress Cataloging-in-Publication Data

Title: Happiness.
Other titles: HBR emotional intelligence series.
Description: Boston, Massachusetts : Harvard Business Review Press, [2017]
    Series: HBR emotional intelligence series
Identifiers: LCCN 2016056298 | ISBN 9781633693210 (pbk. : alk. paper)
Subjects: LCSH: Happiness. | Work—Psychological aspects.
Classification: LCC BF575.H27 H362 2017 | DDC 152.4/2—dc23 LC record available at https://lccn.loc.gov/2016056298

ISBN: 978-1-63369-321-0
eISBN: 978-1-63369-322-7

Contents

Contents

Happiness

HBR EMOTIONAL INTELLIGENCE SERIES

1

Happiness Isn't the Absence of Negative Feelings

By Jennifer Moss

Happiness feels intolerably elusive for many of us. Like fog, you can see it from afar, dense and full of shape. But upon approach, its particles loosen, and suddenly it becomes out of reach, even though it's all around you.

We put so much emphasis on the pursuit of happiness, but if you stop and think about it, to pursue is to chase something without a guarantee of ever catching it.

Up until about six years ago, I was fervently and ineffectively chasing happiness. My husband, Jim, and I were living in San Jose, California, with our two-year-old son and a second baby on the way. On paper, our life appeared rosy. Still, I couldn't seem to find the joy. I always felt so guilty about my sadness. My problems were embarrassingly "first world."

Then in September 2009, my world tilted. Jim fell severely ill. He was diagnosed with Swine Flu (H1N1) and West Nile virus, then Guillain-Barré Syndrome, due to his compromised immune system.

Jim never worried about death. I did.

When we were told Jim's illness was letting up, that he'd won this round, we were relieved. When we were told Jim might not walk for some time—likely a year, maybe longer—we were alarmed. We knew this prognosis meant the end of Jim's career as a pro lacrosse player. What we didn't know was how we'd pay the medical bills or how much energy Jim would have for parenting.

With 10 weeks to go until the baby arrived, I had very little time to think and reflect. Jim, on the other hand, *only* had time. He was used to moving at high speeds, both in life and on the field, so minutes passed like hours in the hospital. He was kept busy with physical and occupational therapy, but he was also in need of psychological support.

He put out a note to people in his social networks, asking them for reading suggestions that would help him to mentally heal. Suggestions flowed in. Books and audio tapes were delivered bedside with notes about how they'd "helped so much" after whatever difficulty this person had also experienced but overcame.

Jim would spend his days reading motivational books from Tony Robbins and Oprah or watching TED talks, like Jill Bolte Taylor's "My Stroke of Insight," about the impacts of brain trauma. He would analyze spiritual books by Deepak Chopra and the Dalai Lama. Or review scientific research papers about happiness and gratitude written by researchers Martin Seligman, Shawn Achor, Sonja Lyubomirsky, and many others.

There was a repeated theme throughout all the literature—gratitude. It would weave in and out of the science, the true stories, and the drivers for success. Jim responded by starting a gratitude journal of his own. He got very thankful—thankful for the people who changed his sheets, thankful for the family that would bring him hot meals at dinner. Thankful for the nurse who would encourage him and thankful for the extra attention his rehab team would give him on their own time. (The team once told Jim that they were only putting in extra time because they knew how grateful he was for their efforts.)

He asked that I participate in his approach, and because I wanted to help him to heal so badly and I was seeing how hard it was for him, I tried hard to be in a positive place when I came into his world inside that hospital room. I wasn't always at my best. I sometimes resented that I couldn't break down—but after a while I started to see how rapidly he was getting better. And although our paths weren't congruent, we were making it work. I was "coming around."

It was shaky and scary, but when Jim walked out of the hospital on crutches (he stubbornly refused the wheelchair) only six weeks after he was rushed by ambulance to the ER, we decided there was something more to his healing than just dumb luck.

One of those early books that influenced Jim was Seligman's *Flourish*. A psychologist and former president of the American Psychology Association, Seligman was responsible for defining the term "PERMA," the root of many positive psychology research projects around the world. The acronym stands for the five elements essential to lasting contentment:

- *Positive emotion*: Peace, gratitude, satisfaction, pleasure, inspiration, hope, curiosity, and love fall into this category.

- *Engagement*: Losing ourselves in a task or project provides us with a sense of "disappeared time" because we are so highly engaged.

- *Relationships*: People who have meaningful, positive relationships with others are happier than those who do not.

- *Meaning*: Meaning comes from serving a cause bigger than ourselves. Whether it's a religion or a cause that helps humanity in some way, we all need meaning in our lives.

- *Accomplishment/achievement*: To feel significant life satisfaction, we must strive to better ourselves.

We slowly brought these five tenets back into our lives. Jim returned to Wilfrid Laurier University in Ontario to research neuroscience, and we promptly started up Plasticity Labs to help teach others what we'd learned about the pursuit of happiness. As our lives came to include more empathy, gratitude, and meaning, I stopped feeling sad.

So when I see skepticism directed at the positive psychology movement, I take it personally. Do these critics have a problem with gratitude? Relationships? Meaning? Hope?

Perhaps part of the problem is that we oversimplify happiness in our pop culture and media, which makes it easy to discard as unproven. As Vanessa Buote, a postdoctoral fellow in social psychology, put it to me in an email:

> *One of the misconceptions about happiness is that happiness is being cheerful, joyous, and content all the time; always having a smile on your face. It's not—being happy and leading rich lives is about taking the good with the bad, and learning how to reframe the bad. In fact, in the recent [article in the* Journal of Experimental Psychology*], "Emodiversity and the Emotional Ecosystem," by Harvard [researcher Jordi] Quoidbach, found that experiencing a wide range of*

emotions—both positive and negative—was linked to positive mental and physical well-being.

Not only do we tend to misunderstand what happiness is, we also tend to chase it the wrong way. Shawn Achor, the researcher and corporate trainer who wrote the HBR article "Positive Intelligence," told me that most people think about happiness the wrong way: "The biggest misconception of the happiness industry is that happiness is an end, not a means. We think that if we get what we want, then we'll be happy. But it turns out that our brains actually work in the opposite direction."

Buote agrees: "We sometimes tend to see 'being happy' as the end goal, but we forget that what's really important is the journey; finding out what makes us the happiest and regularly engaging in those activities to help us lead a more fulfilling life."

In other words, we're not happy when we're chasing happiness. We're happiest when we're not thinking about it, when we're enjoying the present moment because we're lost in a meaningful project, working toward a higher goal, or helping someone who needs us.

Healthy positivity doesn't mean cloaking your authentic feelings. Happiness is not the absence of suffering; it's the ability to rebound from it. And happiness is not the same as joy or ecstasy; happiness includes contentment, well-being, and the emotional flexibility to experience a full range of emotions. At our company, some of us have dealt with anxiety and depression. Some have experienced PTSD. Some of us have witnessed severe mental illness in our families, and some of us have not. We openly share. Or we don't—either way is fine. We support tears in the office, if the situation calls for it (in both sorrow and in laughter).

Some people—perhaps looking for a fresh angle— have even argued that happiness is harmful (see, for example, the last two articles in this book). But the point of practicing exercises that help increase mental and emotional fitness is not to learn to paste a smile on your face or wish away your problems. It's to learn how to handle stressors with more resilience through training, just as you would train to run a marathon.

During my time with Jim in the hospital, I watched him change. It happened in subtle ways at first, but then all at once I realized that practicing gratitude and the happiness that comes with it had given me a gift: It gave me back Jim. If happiness is harmful—then I say, bring it on.

JENNIFER MOSS is a cofounder and chief communications officer of Plasticity Labs.

Adapted from content posted on hbr.org on
August 20, 2015 (product #H02AEB).

2

Being Happy at Work Matters

By Annie McKee

People used to believe that you didn't have to be happy at work to succeed. And you didn't need to like the people you worked with, or even share their values. "Work is *not* personal," the thinking went. This is bunk.

My research with dozens of companies and hundreds of people—along with the research conducted by neuroscientists like Richard Davidson and V.S. Ramachandran and scholars such as Shawn Achor— increasingly points to a simple fact: Happy people are better workers. Those who are engaged with their jobs and colleagues work harder—and smarter.

And yet, an alarmingly high number of people aren't engaged. According to a sobering 2013 Gallup report, only 30% of the U.S. workforce *is* engaged. This echoes what I've seen in my work. Not very many people are truly "emotionally and intellectually committed" to their organizations.[1] Far too many couldn't care less about what's happening around them. For them, Wednesday is "hump day" and they're just working to get to Friday. And then there's the other end of the bell curve—the nearly one out of five employees who is actively *disengaged*, according to the same Gallup report. These people are sabotaging projects, backstabbing colleagues, and generally wreaking havoc in their workplaces.

The Gallup report also notes that employee engagement has remained largely constant over the years despite economic ups and downs. Scary: We're not engaged with work, and we haven't been for a long time.

Disengaged, unhappy people aren't any fun to work with and don't add much value; they impact our or-

ganizations (and our economy) in profoundly negative ways. It's even worse when leaders are disengaged because they infect others with their attitude.
Their emotions and mindsets impact others' moods
and performance tremendously. After all, how we feel
is linked to what and how we think. In other words,
thought influences emotion, and emotion influences
thinking.[2]

It's time to finally blow up the myth that feelings don't matter at work. Science is on our side:
There are clear neurological links between feelings,
thoughts, and actions.[3] When we are in the grip of
strong negative emotions, it's like having blinders on.
We focus mostly—sometimes only—on the source of
the pain. We don't process information as well, think
creatively, or make good decisions. Frustration, anger, and stress cause an important part of us to shut
down—the part that's thinking and engaged.[4] Disen-
gagement is a natural neurological and psychological
response to pervasive negative emotions.

But it's not just negative emotions we need to watch out for. Extremely strong positive emotions can have the same effect.[5] Some studies show that too much happiness can make you less creative and prone to engaging in riskier behaviors (think about how we act like fools when we fall in love). On the work front: I've seen groups of people worked up into a frenzy at sales conferences and corporate pep rallies. Little learning or innovation comes out of these meetings. Throw in a lot of alcohol, and you've got a whole host of problems.

If we can agree that our emotional states at work matter, what can we do to increase engagement and improve performance?

Over the past few years, my team at the Teleos Leadership Institute and I have studied dozens of organizations and interviewed thousands of people. The early findings about the links between people's feelings and engagement are fascinating. There are clear similarities in what people say they want and need, no matter where they are from, whom they work for, or what field they're in. We often assume that there are huge differences across industries and around the world, but the research challenges that assumption.

To be fully engaged and happy, virtually everyone tells, we need three things:

1. *A meaningful vision of the future.* When people talked with our research team about what was working and what wasn't in their organizations and what helped or hindered them the most, they talked about *vision.* People want to be able to see the future and know how they fit in. And, as we know from our work with organizational behavior expert Richard Boyatzis on intentional change, people learn and change when they have a personal vision that is linked to an organizational vision.[6] Sadly, far too many leaders don't paint a very compelling

vision of the future, they don't try to link it to people's personal visions, and they don't communicate well. And they lose people as a result.

2. *A sense of purpose.* People want to feel as if their work matters, that their contributions help achieve something really important. And except for those at the tippy top, shareholder value isn't a meaningful goal that excites and engages them. They want to know that they—and their organizations—are doing something big that matters to other people.

3. *Great relationships.* We know that people join an organization and leave a boss.[7] A dissonant relationship with one's boss is downright painful. So too are bad relationships with colleagues. Leaders, managers, and employees have all told us that close, trusting, and supportive relationships are hugely important to their state of mind—and their willingness contribute to a team.

Added up, brain science and organizational research are in fact debunking the old myths: Emotions matter a lot at work. Happiness is important. To be fully engaged, people need vision, meaning, purpose, and resonant relationships.

It's on us as individuals to find ways to live our values at work and build great relationships. And it's on leaders to create an environment where people can thrive. It's simple and it's practical: If you want an engaged workforce, pay attention to how you create a vision, link people's work to your company's larger purpose, and reward individuals who resonate with others.

ANNIE MCKEE is a senior fellow at the University of Pennsylvania, director of the PennCLO executive doctoral program, and the founder of the Teleos Leadership Institute. She is a co-author with Daniel Goleman and Richard Boyatzis of *Primal Leadership*, *Resonant Leadership*, and *Becoming a Resonant Leader*. The ideas in this article are expanded in McKee's latest book, *How to Be Happy at Work*, forthcoming from Harvard Business Review Press.

Notes

1. A. K. Goel et al., "Measuring the Level of Employee Engagement: A Study from the Indian Automobile Sector." *International Journal of Indian Culture and Business Management* 6, no. 1 (2013): 5–21.

2. J. Lite, "*MIND* Reviews: *The Emotional Life of Your Brain*," *Scientific American MIND*, July 1, 2012, http://www.scientificamerican.com/article/mind-reviews-the-emotional-life-of/.

3. D. Goleman, *Destructive Emotions: A Scientific Dialogue with the Dalai Lama.* (New York: Bantam, 2004).

4. D. Goleman et al., *Primal Leadership: Unleashing the Power of Emotional Intelligence.* (Boston: Harvard Business Review Press, 2013).

5. J. Gruber, "Four Ways Happiness Can Hurt You," *Greater Good*, May 3, 2012, http://greatergood.berkeley.edu/article/item/four_ways_happiness_can_hurt_you.

6. R. E. Boyatzis and C. Soler, "Vision, Leadership, and Emotional Intelligence Transforming Family Business," *Journal of Family Business Management* 2, no. 1 (2012) 23–30; and A. McKee et al., *Becoming a Resonant Leader: Develop Your Emotional Intelligence, Renew Your Relationships, Sustain Your Effectiveness.* (Boston: Harvard Business Review Press, 2008). http://www.amazon.com/Becoming-Resonant-Leader-Relationships-Effectiveness/dp/1422117340.

7. "How Managers Trump Companies," *Gallup Business Journal*, August 12, 1999, http://businessjournal.gallup .com/content/523/how-managers-trump-companies.aspx.

Adapted from content posted on hbr.org on
November 14, 2014 (product #H012CE).

3

The Science Behind the Smile

An interview with Daniel Gilbert by Gardiner Morse

arvard psychology professor Daniel Gilbert is widely known for his 2006 best seller, *Stumbling on Happiness*. His work reveals, among other things, the systematic mistakes we all make in imagining how happy (or miserable) we'll be. In this edited interview with HBR's Gardiner Morse, Gilbert surveys the field of happiness research and explores its frontiers.

HBR: *Happiness research has become a hot topic in the past 20 years. Why?*

Gilbert: It's only recently that we realized we could marry one of our oldest questions—"What is the nature of human happiness?"—to our newest way of getting answers: science. Until just a few decades ago, the problem of happiness was mainly in the hands of philosophers and poets.

Psychologists have always been interested in emotion, but in the past two decades the study of emotion has exploded, and one of the emotions that psychologists have studied most intensively is happiness. Recently economists and neuroscientists joined the party. All these disciplines have distinct but intersecting interests: Psychologists want to understand what people feel, economists want to know what people value, and neuroscientists want to know how people's brains respond to rewards. Having three separate disciplines all interested in a single topic has put that topic on the scientific map. Papers on happiness are published in *Science*, people who study happiness win Nobel prizes, and governments all over the world are rushing to figure out how to measure and increase the happiness of their citizens.

How is it possible to measure something as subjective as happiness?

Measuring subjective experiences is a lot easier than you think. It's what your eye doctor does when she fits you for glasses. She puts a lens in front of your eye and asks you to report your experience, and then she puts another lens up, and then another. She uses your reports as data, submits the data to scientific analysis, and designs a lens that will give you perfect vision—all on the basis of your reports of your subjective experience. People's real-time reports are very good approximations of their experiences, and they make it possible for us to see the world through their eyes. People may not be able to tell us how happy they were yesterday or how happy they will be tomorrow, but they *can* tell us how they're feeling at the moment we ask them. "How are you?" may be the world's most frequently asked question, and nobody's stumped by it.

There are many ways to measure happiness. We can ask people "How happy are you right now?" and have them rate it on a scale. We can use magnetic resonance imaging to measure cerebral blood flow, or electromyography to measure the activity of the "smile muscles" in the face. But in most circumstances those measures are highly correlated, and you'd have to be the federal government to prefer the complicated, expensive measures over the simple, inexpensive one.

But isn't the scale itself subjective? Your five might be my six.

Imagine that a drugstore sold a bunch of cheap thermometers that weren't very well calibrated. People with normal temperatures might get readings other than 98.6, and two people with the same temperature might get different readings. These inaccuracies could cause people to seek medical treatment they didn't need or to miss getting treatment they did need. So buggy thermometers are sometimes a problem—but not always. For example, if I brought 100 people to my lab, exposed half of them to a flu virus, and then used those buggy thermometers to take their temperatures a week later, the average temperature of the people who'd been exposed would almost surely be higher than the average temperature of the others. Some thermometers would underestimate, some would overestimate, but as long as I measured enough people, the inaccuracies would cancel themselves out. Even with poorly calibrated instruments, we can compare large groups of people.

A rating scale is like a buggy thermometer. Its inaccuracies make it inappropriate for some kinds of measurement (for example, saying exactly how happy John was at 10:42 am on July 3, 2010), but it's perfectly appropriate for the kinds of measurements most psychological scientists make.

What did all these happiness researchers discover?

Much of the research confirms things we've always suspected. For example, in general people who are in good romantic relationships are happier than those who aren't. Healthy people are happier than sick people. People who participate in their churches are happier than those who don't. Rich people are happier than poor people. And so on.

That said, there have been some surprises. For example, while all these things do make people happier, it's astonishing how little any one of them matters. Yes, a new house or a new spouse will make you happier, but not much and not for long. As it turns out, people are not very good at predicting what will make them happy or how long that happiness will last. They expect positive events to make them much happier than those events actually do, and they expect negative events to make them unhappier than they actually do. In both field and lab studies, we've found that winning or losing an election, gaining or losing a romantic partner, getting or not getting a promotion, passing or failing an exam all have less impact on happiness than people think they will. A recent study showed that very few experiences affect us for more than three months. When good things happen, we celebrate for a while and then sober up. When bad things happen, we weep and whine for a while and then pick ourselves up and get on with it.

Why do events have such a fleeting effect on happiness?

One reason is that people are good at synthesizing happiness—at finding silver linings. As a result, they usually end up happier than they expect after almost any kind of trauma or tragedy. Pick up any newspaper, and you'll find plenty of examples. Remember Jim Wright, who resigned in disgrace as

Speaker of the House of Representatives because of a shady book deal? A few years later he told the *New York Times* that he was "so much better off, physically, financially, emotionally, mentally and in almost every other way." Then there's Moreese Bickham, who spent 37 years in the Louisiana State Penitentiary; after his release he said, "I don't have one minute's regret. It was a glorious experience." These guys appear to be living in the best of all possible worlds. Speaking of which, Pete Best, the original drummer for the Beatles, was replaced by Ringo Starr in 1962, just before the Beatles got big. Now he's a session drummer. What did he have to say about missing out on the chance to belong to the most famous band of the 20th century? "I'm happier than I would have been with the Beatles."

One of the most reliable findings of the happiness studies is that we do not have to go running to a therapist every time our shoelaces break. We have a remarkable ability to make the best of things. Most people are more resilient than they realize.

Aren't they deluding themselves? Isn't real happiness better than synthetic happiness?

Let's be careful with terms. Nylon is real; it's just not natural. Synthetic happiness is perfectly real; it's just man-made. Synthetic happiness is what we produce when we don't get what we want, and natural happiness is what we experience when we do. They have different origins, but they are not necessarily different in terms of how they feel. One is not obviously better than the other.

Of course, most folks don't see it that way. Most folks think that synthetic happiness isn't as "good" as the other kind—that people who produce it are just fooling themselves and aren't really happy. I know of no evidence demonstrating that that's the case. If you go blind or lose a fortune, you'll find that there's a whole new life on the other side of those events. And you'll find many things about that new life that are quite good. In fact, you'll undoubtedly find a few things that are even better than what you had before. You're not lying to yourself; you're not delusional. You're discovering things you didn't know—*couldn't* know—until you were in that new life. You are looking for things that make your new life better, you are finding them, and they are making you happy. What is most striking to me as a scientist is that most of us don't realize how good we're going to be at finding these things. We'd never say, "Oh, of course, if I lost my money or my wife left me, I'd find a way to be just as happy as I am now." We'd never say it—but it's true.

Is being happy always desirable? Look at all the unhappy creative geniuses—Beethoven, van Gogh, Hemingway. Doesn't a certain amount of unhappiness spur good performance?

Nonsense! Everyone can think of a historical example of someone who was both miserable and creative, but that doesn't mean misery generally promotes creativity. There's certainly someone out there who smoked two packs of cigarettes a day and lived to be 90, but that doesn't mean cigarettes are good for you. The difference between using anecdotes to prove a point and using science to prove a point is that in science you can't just cherry-pick the story that suits you best. You have to examine *all* the stories, or at least take a fair sample of them, and see if there are more miserable creatives or happy creatives, more miserable noncreatives or happy noncreatives. If misery promoted creativity, you'd see a higher percentage of creatives among the miserable than among the delighted. And you don't. By and large, happy people are more creative and more productive. Has there ever been a human being whose misery was the source of his creativity? Of course. But that person is the exception, not the rule.

Many managers would say that contented people aren't the most productive employees, so you want to keep people a little uncomfortable, maybe a little anxious, about their jobs.

Managers who collect data instead of relying on intuition don't say that. I know of no data showing that anxious, fearful employees are more creative or productive. Remember, contentment doesn't mean sitting and staring at the wall. That's what people do when they're bored, and people *hate* being bored. We know that people are happiest when they're appropriately challenged—when they're trying to achieve goals that are difficult but not out of reach. Challenge and threat are not the same thing. People blossom when challenged and wither when threatened. Sure, you can get results from threats: Tell someone, "If you don't get this to me by Friday, you're fired," and you'll probably have it by Friday. But you'll also have an employee who will thereafter do his best to undermine you, who will feel no loyalty to the organization, and who will never do more than he must. It would be much more effective to tell your employee, "I don't think most people could get this done by Friday. But I have full faith and confidence that you can. And it's hugely important to the entire team." Psychologists have studied reward and punishment for a century, and the bottom line is perfectly clear: Reward works better.

So challenge makes people happy. What else do we know now about the sources of happiness?

If I had to summarize all the scientific literature on the causes of human happiness in one word, that word would be "social." We are by far the most social species on Earth. Even ants have nothing on us. If I wanted to predict your happiness, and I could know only one thing about you, I wouldn't want to know your gender, religion, health, or income. I'd want to know about your social network—about your friends and family and the strength of your bonds with them.

Beyond having rich networks, what makes us happy day to day?

The psychologist Ed Diener has a finding I really like. He essentially shows that the *frequency* of your positive experiences is a much better predictor of your happiness than is the *intensity* of your positive experiences. When we think about what would make us happy, we tend to think of intense events—going on a date with a movie star, winning a Pulitzer, buying a yacht. But Diener and his colleagues have shown that how good your experiences are doesn't matter nearly as much as how many good experiences you have. Somebody who has a dozen mildly nice things happen each day is likely to be happier than somebody who has a single truly amazing thing happen. So wear comfortable shoes, give your wife a big kiss, sneak a french fry. It sounds like small stuff, and it is. But the small stuff matters.

I think this helps explain why it's so hard for us to forecast our affective states. We imagine that one or two big things will have a profound effect. But it looks like happiness is the sum of hundreds of small things. Achieving happiness requires the same approach as losing weight. People trying to lose weight want a magic pill that will give them instant results. Ain't no such thing. We know exactly how people lose weight: They eat less and exercise more. They don't have to eat *much* less or exercise *much* more— they just have to do those things consistently. Over time it adds up. Happiness is like that. The things you can do to increase your happiness are obvious and small and take just a little time. But you have to do them every day and wait for the results.

What are those little things we can do to increase our happiness?

They won't surprise you any more than "eat less and exercise more" does. The main things are to commit to some simple behaviors—meditating, exercising, getting enough sleep—and to practice altruism. One of the most selfish things you can do is help others. Volunteer at a homeless shelter. You may or may not help the homeless, but you will almost surely help yourself. And nurture your social connections. Twice a week, write down three things you're grateful for, and tell someone why. I know these sound like homilies from your grandmother. Well, your grandmother was smart. The secret of happiness is like the secret of weight loss: It's not a secret!

If there's no secret, what's left to study?

There's no shortage of questions. For decades psychologists and economists have been asking,

"Who's happy? The rich? The poor? The young? The old?" The best we could do was divide people into groups, survey them once or maybe twice, and try to determine if the people in one group were, on average, happier than those in the others. The tools we used were pretty blunt instruments. But now millions of people are carrying little computers in their pockets—smartphones—and this allows us to collect data in real time from huge numbers of people about what they are doing and feeling from moment to moment. That's never been possible before.

One of my collaborators, Matt Killingsworth, has built an experience-sampling application called Track Your Happiness. He follows more than 15,000 people by iPhone, querying them several times a day about their activities and emotional states. Are they at home? On a bus? Watching television? Praying? How are they feeling? What are they thinking about? With this technology, Matt's beginning to answer a much better

question than the one we've been asking for decades. Instead of asking *who* is happy, he can ask
when they are happy. He doesn't get the answer by
asking, "When are you happy?"—because frankly,
people don't know. He gets it by tracking people
over days, months, and years and measuring what
they are doing and how happy they are while they
are doing it. I think this kind of technology is
about to revolutionize our understanding of daily
emotions and human well-being. (See the sidebar
"The Future of Happiness Research.")

What are the new frontiers of happiness research?

We need to get more specific about what we are
measuring. Many scientists say they are studying
happiness, but when you look at what they're measuring, you find they are actually studying depression or life satisfaction. These things are related
to happiness, of course, but they are not the same
as happiness. Research shows that people with

children are typically less happy on a moment-to-moment basis than people without children. But people who have kids may feel fulfilled in a way that people without kids do not. It doesn't make sense to say that people with kids are happier, or that people without kids are happier; each group is happier in some ways and less happy in others. We need to stop painting our portrait of happiness with such a fat brush.

Will all this research ultimately make us happier?

We are learning and will continue to learn how to maximize our happiness. So yes, there is no doubt that the research has helped and will continue to help us increase our happiness. But that still leaves the big question: What kind of happiness *should* we want? For example, do we want the average happiness of our moments to be as large as possible, or do we want the sum of our happy moments to be as large as possible? Those are different things.

Do we want lives free of pain and heartache, or is there value in those experiences? Science will soon be able to tell us how to live the lives we want, but it will never tell us what kinds of lives we should want to live. That will be for us to decide.

THE FUTURE OF HAPPINESS RESEARCH

by Matthew Killingsworth

You'd think it would be easy to figure out what makes us happy. Until recently, though, researchers have had to rely mainly on people's reports about their average emotional states over long periods of time and on easily surveyed predictors of happiness, such as demographic variables. As a result, we know that married or wealthy people are, on average, happier than unmarried or less-well-off people. But what is it about being married or having money that makes people happy?

Focusing on average emotional states also smoothes out short-term fluctuations in happiness and consequently diminishes our ability to understand the causes of those fluctuations. For example, how do the moment-by-moment details of a person's day affect that person's happiness?

We can now begin to answer questions like these, thanks to the smartphone. For an ongoing research project called Track Your Happiness, I have recruited more than 15,000 people in 83 countries to report their emotional states in real time, using devices they carry with them every day. I created an iPhone web app that queries users at random intervals, asking them about their mood (respondents slide a button along a scale that ranges from "very bad" to "very good"), what they are doing (they can select from 22 options, including commuting, working, exercising,

(Continued)

47

and eating), and factors such as their level of productivity, the nature of their environment, the amount and quality of their sleep, and their social interactions. Since 2009 we have collected more than half a million data points—making this, to my knowledge, the first-ever large-scale study of happiness in daily life.

One major finding is that people's minds wander nearly half the time, and this appears to lower their mood. Wandering to unpleasant or even neutral topics is associated with sharply lower happiness; straying to positive topics has no effect either way. The amount of mind-wandering varies greatly depending on the activity, from roughly 60% of the time while commuting to 30% when talking to someone or playing a game to 10% during sex. But no matter what people are doing, they are much less happy when their minds are wandering than when their minds are focused.

All of this strongly suggests that to optimize our emotional well-being, we should pay at least as much attention to where our minds are as to what our bodies are doing. Yet for most of us, the focus of our thoughts isn't part of our daily planning. When you wake up on a Saturday morning and ask, "What am I going to do today?" the answer is usually about where you'll take your body—to the beach, to the kids' soccer practice, for a run. You ought to also ask, "What am I going to do with my mind today?"

A related stream of research examines the relationship between mind-wandering and productivity. Many managers, particularly those whose employees do creative knowledge work, may sense that a certain amount of daydreaming is a good thing, providing a mental break and perhaps leading people to reflect on related work matters. Unfortunately, the data so far suggest that, in addition to reducing happiness, mind-wandering on the job reduces productivity. And employees' minds stray much more than managers

(Continued)

probably imagine—about 50% of the workday—and almost always veer toward personal concerns. Managers may want to look for ways to help employees stay focused, for the employees' *and* the company's sakes.

The data are also beginning to paint a picture of variations in happiness within an individual and from one individual to the next. The most striking finding here is that happiness differs more from moment to moment than it does from person to person. This suggests that it's not the stable conditions of our lives, such as where we live or whether we're married, that are the principal drivers of happiness; it could be the small, everyday things that count the most.

It also suggests that happiness on the job may depend more on our moment-to-moment experiences— our routine interactions with coworkers, the projects we're involved in, our daily contributions—than on the

A focused mind is a happy mind

Participants were queried about mood and mind-wandering during 22 activities. The balls represent their activities and thoughts. The farther to the right a ball is, the happier people were, on average. The larger the ball, the more frequently they engaged in the activity or thought.

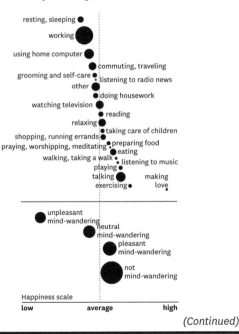

(Continued)

51

stable conditions thought to promote happiness, such as a high salary or a prestigious title. A priority of my current and future research is to deploy this tracking technology in the workplace and, I hope, at last reveal what actually makes employees happy.

Matthew Killingsworth is a doctoral student in psychology at Harvard University. He is the creator of www.trackyour happiness.com.

DANIEL GILBERT is the Edgar Pierce Professor of Psychology at Harvard University. He has won numerous awards for his research and teaching, including the American Psychological Association's Distinguished Scientific Award for an Early Career Contribution to Psychology. He is the author of *Stumbling on Happiness* and host and co-writer of the PBS television series *This Emotional Life*. GARDINER MORSE is a senior editor at *Harvard Business Review*.

Reprinted from *Harvard Business Review*, January–February 2012 (product #R1201E).

4

The Power of
Small Wins

By Teresa M. Amabile and Steven J. Kramer

What is the best way to drive innovative work inside organizations? Important clues hide in the stories of world-renowned creators. It turns out that ordinary scientists, marketers, programmers, and other unsung knowledge workers, whose jobs require creative productivity every day, have more in common with famous innovators than most managers realize. The workday events that ignite their emotions, fuel their motivation, and trigger their perceptions are fundamentally the same.

The Double Helix, James Watson's 1968 memoir about discovering the structure of DNA, describes the roller coaster of emotions he and Francis Crick experienced through the progress and setbacks of the work that eventually earned them the Nobel Prize. After the excitement of their first attempt to build a DNA model, Watson and Crick noticed some serious flaws. According to Watson, "Our first minutes with the models . . . were not joyous." Later that evening, "a shape began to emerge which brought back our spirits." But when they showed their "breakthrough" to colleagues, they found that their model would not work. Dark days of doubt and ebbing motivation followed. When the duo finally had their bona fide breakthrough, and their colleagues found no fault with it, Watson wrote, "My morale skyrocketed, for I suspected that we now had the answer to the riddle." Watson and Crick were so driven by this success that they practically lived in the lab, trying to complete the work.

Throughout these episodes, Watson and Crick's progress—or lack thereof—ruled their reactions. In our recent research on creative work inside businesses, we stumbled upon a remarkably similar phenomenon. Through exhaustive analysis of diaries kept by knowledge workers, we discovered the "progress principle": Of all the things that can boost emotions, motivation, and perceptions during a workday, the single most important is making progress in meaningful work. And the more frequently people experience that sense of progress, the more likely they are to be creatively productive in the long run. Whether they are trying to solve a major scientific mystery or simply produce a high-quality product or service, everyday progress—even a small win—can make all the difference in how they feel and perform.

The power of progress is fundamental to human nature, but few managers understand it or know how to leverage progress to boost motivation. In fact, work motivation has been a subject of long-standing debate. In a survey asking about the keys to motivating workers, we found that some managers ranked recognition for good work as most important, while others put more stock in tangible incentives. Some focused on the value of interpersonal support, while still others thought clear goals were the answer. Interestingly, very few of our surveyed managers ranked progress first. (See the sidebar "A Surprise for Managers.")

If you are a manager, the progress principle holds clear implications for where to focus your efforts. It suggests that you have more influence than you may realize over employees' well-being, motivation, and creative output. Knowing what serves to catalyze and nourish progress—and what does the opposite—turns out to be the key to effectively managing people and their work.

In this article, we share what we have learned about the power of progress and how managers can leverage it. We spell out how a focus on progress translates into concrete managerial actions and pro-vide a checklist to help make such behaviors habitual. But to clarify why those actions are so potent, we first

A SURPRISE FOR MANAGERS

In a 1968 issue of HBR, Frederick Herzberg published a now-classic article titled "One More Time: How Do you Motivate Employees?" Our findings are consistent with his message: People are most satisfied with their jobs (and therefore most motivated) when those jobs give them the opportunity to experience achievement. The diary research we describe in this article—in which we microscopically examined the events of thousands of workdays, in real time—uncovered the mechanism underlying the sense of achievement: making consistent, meaningful progress.

But managers seem not to have taken Herzberg's lesson to heart. To assess contemporary awareness of the importance of daily work progress, we recently administered a survey to 669 managers of varying levels from dozens of companies around the world. We asked about the managerial tools that can affect employees'

(Continued)

motivation and emotions. The respondents ranked five tools—support for making progress in the work, recognition for good work, incentives, interpersonal support, and clear goals—in order of importance.

Of the managers who took our survey, 95% would probably be surprised to learn that supporting progress is the primary way to elevate motivation—because that's the percentage who failed to rank progress number one. In fact, only 35 managers ranked progress as the number one motivator—a mere 5%. The vast majority of respondents ranked support for making progress dead last as a motivator and third as an influence on emotion. They ranked "recognition for good work (either public or private)" as the most important factor in motivating workers and making them happy. In our diary study, recognition certainly did boost inner work life. But it wasn't nearly as prominent as progress. Besides, without work achievements, there is little to recognize.

describe our research and what the knowledge workers' diaries revealed about their "inner work lives."

Inner work life and performance

For nearly 15 years, we have been studying the psychological experiences and the performance of people doing complex work inside organizations. Early on, we realized that a central driver of creative, productive performance was the quality of a person's inner work life: the mix of emotions, motivations, and perceptions over the course of a workday. How happy workers feel; how motivated they are by an intrinsic interest in the work; how positively they view their organization, their management, their team, their work, and themselves—all these combine either to push them to higher levels of achievement or to drag them down.

To understand such interior dynamics better, we asked members of project teams to respond individually to an end-of-day email survey during the course of the project—just over four months, on average. (For more on this research, see our article "Inner Work Life: Understanding the Subtext of Business Performance," HBR May 2007.) The projects—inventing kitchen gadgets, managing product lines of cleaning tools, and solving complex IT problems for a hotel empire, for example—all involved creativity. The daily survey inquired about participants' emotions and moods, motivation levels, and perceptions of the work environment that day, as well as what work they did and what events stood out in their minds.

Twenty-six project teams from seven companies participated, comprising 238 individuals. This yielded nearly 12,000 diary entries. Naturally, every individual in our population experienced ups and downs. Our goal was to discover the states of inner work life and the workday events that correlated with the highest levels of creative output.

In a dramatic rebuttal to the commonplace claim that high pressure and fear spur achievement, we found that, at least in the realm of knowledge work, people are more creative and productive when their inner work lives are positive—when they feel happy, are intrinsically motivated by the work itself, and have positive perceptions of their colleagues and the organization. Moreover, in those positive states, people are more committed to the work and more collegial toward those around them. Inner work life, we saw, can fluctuate from one day to the next— sometimes wildly—and performance along with it. A person's inner work life on a given day fuels his or her performance for the day and can even affect performance the *next* day.

Once this "inner work-life effect" became clear, our inquiry turned to whether and how managerial action could set it in motion. What events could evoke positive or negative emotions, motivations, and perceptions? The answers were tucked within our research participants' diary entries. There are predictable triggers that inflate or deflate inner work life, and, even accounting for variation among individuals, they are pretty much the same for everyone.

The power of progress

Our hunt for inner work-life triggers led us to the progress principle. When we compared our research participants' best and worst days (based on their overall mood, specific emotions, and motivation levels), we found that the most common event triggering a "best day" was any progress in the work by the individual or the team. The most common event triggering a "worst day" was a setback.

Consider, for example, how progress relates to one component of inner work life: overall mood ratings. Steps forward occurred on 76% of people's best-mood days. By contrast, setbacks occurred on only 13% of those days. (See the figure "What happens on good days and bad days?")

Two other types of inner work-life triggers also occur frequently on best days: *catalysts*, actions that directly support work, including help from a person or group, and *nourishers*, events such as shows of respect and words of encouragement. Each has an opposite: *inhibitors*, actions that fail to support or actively hinder work, and *toxins*, discouraging or undermining events. Whereas catalysts and inhibitors are directed at the project, nourishers and toxins are directed at the person. Like setbacks, inhibitors and toxins are rare on days of great inner work life.

Events on worst-mood days are nearly the mirror image of those on best-mood days. Here, setbacks predominated, occurring on 67% of those days; progress occurred on only 25% of them. Inhibitors and toxins also marked many worst-mood days, and catalysts and nourishers were rare.

This is the progress principle made visible: If a person is motivated and happy at the end of a workday, it's a good bet that he or she made some progress.

If the person drags out of the office disengaged and joyless, a setback is most likely to blame.

When we analyzed all 12,000 daily surveys filled out by our participants, we discovered that progress and setbacks influence all three aspects of inner work life. On days when they made progress, our participants reported more positive *emotions*. They not only were in a more upbeat mood in general but also expressed more joy, warmth, and pride. When they suffered setbacks, they experienced more frustration, fear, and sadness.

Motivations were also affected: On progress days, people were more intrinsically motivated—by interest in and enjoyment of the work itself. On setback days, they were not only less intrinsically motivated but also less extrinsically motivated by recognition. Apparently, setbacks can lead a person to feel generally apathetic and disinclined to do the work at all.

Perceptions differed in many ways, too. On progress days, people perceived significantly more positive

What happens on good days and bad days?

Progress—even a small step forward—occurs on many of the days people report being in a good mood. Events on bad days—setbacks and other hindrances—are nearly the mirror image of those on good days.

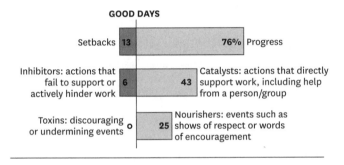

GOOD DAYS

Setbacks **13** — **76%** Progress

Inhibitors: actions that fail to support or actively hinder work **6** — **43** Catalysts: actions that directly support work, including help from a person/group

Toxins: discouraging or undermining events **o** — **25** Nourishers: events such as shows of respect or words of encouragement

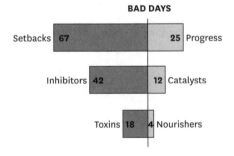

BAD DAYS

Setbacks **67** — **25** Progress

Inhibitors **42** — **12** Catalysts

Toxins **18** — **4** Nourishers

challenge in their work. They saw their teams as more mutually supportive and reported more positive interactions between the teams and their supervisors. On a number of dimensions, perceptions suffered when people encountered setbacks. They found less positive challenge in the work, felt that they had less freedom in carrying it out, and reported that they had insufficient resources. On setback days, participants perceived both their teams and their supervisors as less supportive.

To be sure, our analyses establish correlations but do not prove causality. Were these changes in inner work life the result of progress and setbacks, or was the effect the other way around? The numbers alone cannot answer that. However, we do know, from reading thousands of diary entries, that more-positive perceptions, a sense of accomplishment, satisfaction, happiness, and even elation often followed progress. Here's a typical post-progress entry, from a programmer: "I smashed that bug that's been frustrating me for almost a calendar week. That may not be an event to you, but I live a very drab life, so I'm all hyped."

Likewise, we saw that deteriorating perceptions, frustration, sadness, and even disgust often followed setbacks. As another participant, a product marketer, wrote, "We spent a lot of time updating the cost reduction project list, and after tallying all the numbers, we are still coming up short of our goal. It is discouraging to not be able to hit it after all the time spent and hard work."

Almost certainly, the causality goes both ways, and managers can use this feedback loop between progress and inner work life to support both.

Minor milestones

When we think about progress, we often imagine how good it feels to achieve a long-term goal or experience a major breakthrough. These big wins are great—but they are relatively rare. The good news is that even small wins can boost inner work life tremendously. Many of the progress events our research participants reported represented only minor steps forward. Yet they often evoked outsize positive reactions. Consider this diary entry from a programmer in a high-tech company, which was accompanied by very positive self-ratings of her emotions, motivations, and perceptions that day: "I figured out why something was not working correctly. I felt relieved and happy because this was a minor milestone for me."

Even ordinary, incremental progress can increase people's engagement in the work and their happiness during the workday. Across all the types of events our participants reported, a notable proportion (28%) that had a minor impact on the project had a major impact on people's feelings about it. Because inner work life has such a potent effect on creativity and productivity, and because small but consistent steps forward shared by many people can accumulate into excellent execution, progress events that often go unnoticed are critical to the overall performance of organizations.

Unfortunately, there is a flip side. Small losses or setbacks can have an extremely negative effect on inner work life. In fact, our study and research by others show that negative events can have a more powerful impact than positive ones. Consequently, it is especially important for managers to minimize daily hassles. (See again the figure "What happens on good days and bad days?")

Progress in meaningful work

We've shown how gratifying it is for workers when they are able to chip away at a goal, but recall what we said earlier: The key to motivating performance is supporting progress in *meaningful* work. Making headway boosts your inner work life, but only if the work matters to you.

Think of the most boring job you've ever had. Many people nominate their first job as a teenager—washing pots and pans in a restaurant kitchen, for example, or checking coats at a museum. In jobs like those, the power of progress seems elusive. No matter how hard you work, there are always more pots to wash and coats to check; only punching the time clock at the end of the day or getting the paycheck at the end of the week yields a sense of accomplishment.

In jobs with much more challenge and room for creativity, like the ones our research participants had, simply "making progress"—getting tasks done—doesn't guarantee a good inner work life, either. You may have experienced this rude fact in your own job, on days (or in projects) when you felt demotivated, devalued, and frustrated, even though you worked hard and got things done. The likely cause is your perception of the completed tasks as peripheral or irrelevant. For the progress principle to operate, the work must be meaningful to the person doing it.

In 1983, Steve Jobs was trying to entice John Sculley to leave a wildly successful career at PepsiCo to become Apple's new CEO. Jobs reportedly asked him, "Do you want to spend the rest of your life selling sugared water or do you want a chance to change the world?" In making his pitch, Jobs leveraged a potent psychological force: the deep-seated human desire to do meaningful work.

Fortunately, to feel meaningful, work doesn't have to involve putting the first personal computers in the hands of ordinary people, or alleviating poverty, or helping to cure cancer. Work with less profound importance to society can matter if it contributes value to something or someone important to the worker. Meaning can be as simple as making a useful and high-quality product for a customer or providing a genuine service for a community. It can be supporting a colleague or boosting an organization's profits by reducing inefficiencies in a production process. Whether the goals are lofty or modest, as long as they are meaningful to the worker and it is clear how his or her efforts contribute to them, progress toward them can galvanize inner work life.

In principle, managers shouldn't have to go to extraordinary lengths to infuse jobs with meaning. Most jobs in modern organizations are potentially meaningful for the people doing them. However, managers can make sure that employees know just how their work is contributing. And, most important, they can avoid actions that negate its value. (See the sidebar "How Work Gets Stripped of Its Meaning.") All the participants in our research were doing work that should have been meaningful; no one was washing pots or checking coats. Shockingly often, however, we saw potentially important, challenging work losing its power to inspire.

HOW WORK GETS STRIPPED OF ITS MEANING

Diary entries from 238 knowledge workers who were members of creative project teams revealed four primary ways in which managers unwittingly drain work of its meaning.

Managers may dismiss the importance of employees' work or ideas. Consider the case of Richard, a senior lab technician at a chemical company, who found meaning in helping his new-product development team solve complex technical problems. However, in team meetings over the course of a three-week period, Richard perceived that his team leader was ignoring his suggestions and those of his teammates. As a result, he felt that his contributions were not meaningful, and his spirits flagged. When at last he believed that he was again making a substantive contribution to the success of the project, his mood

(Continued)

improved dramatically: "I felt much better at today's team meeting. I felt that my opinions and information were important to the project and that we have made some progress."

They may destroy employees' sense of ownership of their work. Frequent and abrupt reassignments often have this effect. This happened repeatedly to the members of a product development team in a giant consumer products company, as described by team member Bruce: "As I've been handing over some projects, I do realize that I don't like to give them up. Especially when you have been with them from the start and are nearly to the end. You lose ownership. This happens to us way too often."

Managers may send the message that the work employees are doing will never see the light of day. They can signal this—unintentionally—by shifting their priorities or changing their minds about how something should be done. We saw the latter in an internet technology company after user-interface developer Burt had spent weeks designing seamless transitions for non-English-speaking users. Not surprisingly, Burt's mood was seriously marred on the day he reported this incident: "Other options for the international [interfaces] were [given] to the team during a team meeting, which could render the work I am doing useless."

They may neglect to inform employees about unexpected changes in a customer's priorities. Often, this arises from poor customer management or inadequate communication within the company. For example, Stuart, a data transformation expert at an IT company, reported deep frustration and low

(Continued)

motivation on the day he learned that weeks of the team's hard work might have been for naught: "Found out that there is a strong possibility that the project may not be going forward, due to a shift in the client's agenda. Therefore, there is a strong possibility that all the time and effort put into the project was a waste of our time."

Supporting progress: catalysts and nourishers

What can managers do to ensure that people are motivated, committed, and happy? How can they support workers' daily progress? They can use catalysts and nourishers, the other kinds of frequent "best day" events we discovered.

Catalysts are actions that support work. They include setting clear goals, allowing autonomy, providing sufficient resources and time, helping with the work, openly learning from problems and successes, and allowing a free exchange of ideas. Their opposites, inhibitors, include failing to provide support and actively interfering with the work. Because of their impact on progress, catalysts and inhibitors ultimately affect inner work life. But they also have a more immediate impact: When people realize that they have clear and meaningful goals, sufficient resources, helpful colleagues, and so on, they get an instant boost to their emotions, their motivation to do a great job, and their perceptions of the work and the organization.

Nourishers are acts of interpersonal support, such as respect and recognition, encouragement, emotional comfort, and opportunities for affiliation. Toxins, their opposites, include disrespect, discouragement, disregard for emotions, and interpersonal conflict. For good and for ill, nourishers and toxins affect inner work life directly and immediately.

Catalysts and nourishers—and their opposites—can alter the meaningfulness of work by shifting people's perceptions of their jobs and even themselves. For instance, when a manager makes sure that people have the resources they need, it signals to them that what they are doing is important and valuable. When managers recognize people for the work they do, it signals that they are important to the organization. In this way, catalysts and nourishers can lend greater meaning to the work—and amplify the operation of the progress principle.

The managerial actions that constitute catalysts and nourishers are not particularly mysterious; they may sound like Management 101, if not just common sense and common decency. But our diary study reminded us how often they are ignored or forgotten. Even some of the more attentive managers in the companies we studied did not consistently provide catalysts and nourishers. For example, a supply chain specialist named Michael was, in many ways and on most days, an excellent subteam manager. But he was occasionally so overwhelmed that he became toxic toward his people. When a supplier failed to complete a "hot" order on time and Michael's team had to resort to air shipping to meet the customer's deadline, he realized that the profit margin on the sale would be blown. In irritation, he lashed out at his subordinates, demeaning the solid work they had done and disregarding their own frustration with the supplier. In his diary, he admitted as much: "As of Friday, we have spent $28,000 in air freight to send 1,500 $30 spray jet mops to our number two customer. Another 2,800 remain on this order, and there is a good probability that they too will gain wings. I have turned from the kindly supply chain manager into the black-masked executioner. All similarity to civility is gone, our backs are against the wall, flight is not possible, therefore fight is probable."

Even when managers don't have their backs against the wall, developing long-term strategy and launching new initiatives can often seem more important—and perhaps sexier—than making sure subordinates have what they need to make steady progress and feel supported as human beings. But as we saw repeatedly in our research, even the best strategy will fail if managers ignore the people working in the trenches to execute it.

A model manager—and a tool for emulating him

We could explain the many (and largely unsurprising) moves that can catalyze progress and nourish spirits, but it may be more useful to give an example of a manager who consistently used those moves—and then to provide a simple tool that can help any manager do so.

Our model manager is Graham, whom we observed leading a small team of chemical engineers within a multinational European firm we'll call Kruger-Bern. The mission of the team's NewPoly project was clear and meaningful enough: Develop a safe, biodegradable polymer to replace petrochemicals in cosmetics and, eventually, in a wide range of consumer products. As in many large firms however, the project was nested in a confusing and sometimes threatening corporate setting of shifting top-management priorities, conflicting signals, and wavering commitments. Resources were uncomfortably tight, and uncertainty loomed over the project's future—and every team member's career. Even worse, an incident early in the project, in which an important customer reacted angrily to a sample, left the team reeling. Yet Graham was able to sustain team members' inner work lives by repeatedly and visibly removing obstacles, materially supporting progress, and emotionally supporting the team.

Graham's management approach excelled in four ways. First, he established a positive climate, one event at a time, which set behavioral norms for the entire team. When the customer complaint stopped the project in its tracks, for example, he engaged immediately with the team to analyze the problem, without recriminations, and develop a plan for repairing the relationship. In doing so, he modeled how to respond to crises in the work: not by panicking or pointing fingers but by identifying problems and their causes and developing a coordinated action plan. This is both a practical approach and a great way to give subordinates a sense of forward movement even in the face of the missteps and failures inherent in any complex project.

Second, Graham stayed attuned to his team's everyday activities and progress. In fact, the nonjudgmental climate he had established made this happen naturally. Team members updated him frequently—

without being asked—on their setbacks, progress, and plans. At one point, one of his hardest-working colleagues, Brady, had to abort a trial of a new material because he couldn't get the parameters right on the equipment. It was bad news, because the New-Poly team had access to the equipment only one day a week, but Brady immediately informed Graham. In his diary entry that evening, Brady noted, "He didn't like the lost week but seemed to understand." That understanding assured Graham's place in the stream of information that would allow him to give his people just what they needed to make progress.

Third, Graham targeted his support according to recent events in the team and the project. Each day, he could anticipate what type of intervention—a catalyst or the removal of an inhibitor; a nourisher or some antidote to a toxin—would have the most impact on team members' inner work lives and progress. And if he could not make that judgment, he asked. Most days it was not hard to figure out, as on the day he received some uplifting news about his bosses' commitment to the project. He knew the team was jittery about a rumored corporate reorganization and could use the encouragement. Even though the clarification came during a well-earned vacation day, he immediately got on the phone to relay the good news to the team.

Finally, Graham established himself as a resource for team members rather than a micromanager; he was sure to check in while never seeming to check *up* on them. Superficially, checking in and checking up seem quite similar, but micromanagers make four kinds of mistakes. First, they fail to allow autonomy in carrying out the work. Unlike Graham, who gave the NewPoly team a clear strategic goal but respected members' ideas about how to meet it, micromanagers dictate every move. Second, they frequently ask subordinates about their work without providing any real help. By contrast, when one of Graham's team members reported problems, Graham helped ana-lyze them—remaining open to alternative interpre-tations—and often ended up helping to get things back on track. Third, micromanagers are quick to affix personal blame when problems arise, leading subordinates to hide problems rather than honestly discuss how to surmount them, as Graham did with Brady. And fourth, micromanagers tend to hoard in-formation to use as a secret weapon. Few realize how damaging this is to inner work life. When subordi-nates perceive that a manager is withholding poten-tially useful information, they feel infantilized, their motivation wanes, and their work is handicapped. Graham was quick to communicate upper manage-ment's views of the project, customers' opinions and needs, and possible sources of assistance or resis-tance within and outside the organization.

In all those ways, Graham sustained his team's positive emotions, intrinsic motivation, and favorable perceptions. His actions serve as a powerful example of how managers at any level can approach each day determined to foster progress.

We know that many managers, however well-intentioned, will find it hard to establish the habits that seemed to come so naturally to Graham. Awareness, of course, is the first step. However, turning an awareness of the importance of inner work life into routine action takes discipline. With that in mind, we developed a checklist for managers to consult on a daily basis (see the sidebar "The Daily Progress Checklist"). The aim of the checklist is managing for meaningful progress, one day at a time.

The progress loop

Inner work life drives performance; in turn, good performance, which depends on consistent progress, enhances inner work life. We call this the "progress loop"—it reveals the potential for self-reinforcing benefits.

So, the most important implication of the progress principle is this: By supporting people and their daily progress in meaningful work, managers improve not only the inner work lives of their employees but also the organization's long-term performance, which enhances inner work life even more. Of course, there is a dark side—the possibility of negative feedback loops. If managers fail to support progress and the people trying to make it, inner work life suffers and so does performance; and degraded performance further undermines inner work life.

A second implication of the progress principle is that managers needn't fret about trying to read the psyches of their workers or manipulate complicated incentive schemes to ensure that employees are motivated and happy. As long as managers show basic respect and consideration, they can focus on supporting the work itself.

To become an effective manager, you must learn to set this positive feedback loop in motion. That may require a significant shift. Business schools, business books, and managers themselves usually focus on managing organizations or people. But if you focus on managing progress, the management of people—and even of entire organizations—becomes much more feasible. You won't have to figure out how to x-ray the inner work lives of subordinates; if you facilitate their steady progress in meaningful work, make that progress salient to them, and treat them well, they will experience the emotions, motivations, and perceptions necessary for great performance. Their superior work will contribute to organizational success. And here's the beauty of it: They will love their jobs.

TERESA M. AMABILE is the Edsel Bryant Ford Professor of Business Administration at Harvard Business School and the author of *Creativity in Context* (Westview Press, 1996). STEVEN J. KRAMER is an independent researcher, writer, and consultant. He is a coauthor of "Creativity Under the Gun" (HBR August 2002) and "Inner Work Life" (HBR May 2007). Amabile and Kramer are the coauthors of *The Progress*

Principle: Using Small Wins to Ignite Joy, Engagement, and Creativity at Work (Harvard Business Review Press, 2011).

Reprinted from *Harvard Business Review*,
May 2011 (product # R1105C).

THE DAILY PROGRESS CHECKLIST

Near the end of each workday, use this checklist to review the day and plan your managerial actions for the next day. After a few days, you will be able to identify issues by scanning the boldface words.

First, focus on progress and setbacks and think about specific events (catalysts, nourishers, inhibitors, and toxins) that contributed to them. Next, consider any clear inner-work-life clues and what further information they provide about progress and other events. Finally, prioritize for action.

The action plan for the next day is the most important part of your daily review: What is the one thing you can do to best facilitate progress?

(Continued)

Progress

Which 1 or 2 events today indicated either a small win or a possible breakthrough? (Describe briefly.)

_____

_____

Catalysts

- ☐ Did the team have clear short- and long-term **goals** for meaningful work?

- ☐ Did team members have sufficient **autonomy** to solve problems and take ownership of the project?

- ☐ Did they have all the **resources** they needed to move forward efficiently?

- ☐ Did they have sufficient **time** to focus on meaningful work?

- ☐ Did I discuss **lessons** from today's successes and problems with my team?

▬▬▬▬▬▬▬▬▬▬▬▬▬▬▬▬

- ☐ Did I give or get them **help** when they needed or requested it? Did I encourage team members to help one another?
- ☐ Did I help **ideas** flow freely within the group?

Nourishers

- ☐ Did I show **respect** to team members by recognizing their contributions to progress, attending to their ideas, and treating them as trusted professionals?
- ☐ Did I **encourage** team members who faced difficult challenges?
- ☐ Did I **support** team members who had a personal or professional problem?
- ☐ Is there a sense of personal and professional **affiliation** and camaraderie within the team?

(Continued)

Setbacks

Which 1 or 2 events today indicated either a small setback or a possible crisis? (Describe briefly.)

_____

_____

Inhibitors

- ☐ Was there any confusion regarding long- or short-term **goals** for meaningful work?

- ☐ Were team members overly **constrained** in their ability to solve problems and feel ownership of the project?

- ☐ Did they lack any of the **resources** they needed to move forward effectively?

- ☐ Did they lack sufficient **time** to focus on meaningful work?

- ☐ Did I or others fail to provide needed or requested **help**?

- ☐ Did I "punish" failure or neglect to find **lessons** and/or opportunities in problems and successes?

- ☐ Did I or others cut off the presentation or debate of **ideas** prematurely?

Toxins

- ☐ Did I **disrespect** any team members by failing to recognize their contributions to progress, not attending to their ideas, or not treating them as trusted professionals?

- ☐ Did I **discourage** a member of the team in any way?

- ☐ Did I **neglect** a team member who had a personal or professional problem?

- ☐ Is there tension or **antagonism** among members of the team or between team members and me?

(Continued)

Inner work life

- Did I see any indications of the quality of my sub-ordinates' inner work lives today? _____

  _____

  _____

- Perceptions of the work, team, management, firm _____

  _____

- Emotions_____

  _____

  _____

- Motivation _____

  _____

- What specific events might have affected inner work life today? _____

  _____

Action plan

- What can I do tomorrow to strengthen the catalysts and nourishers identified and provide the ones that are lacking? _____

  _____

  _____

  _____

  _____

- What can I do tomorrow to start eliminating the inhibitors and toxins identified? _____

  _____

  _____

  _____

  _____

5

Creating Sustainable Performance

By Gretchen Spreitzer and Christine Porath

When the economy's in terrible shape, when any of us is lucky to have a job—let alone one that's financially and intellectually rewarding—worrying about whether or not your employees are happy might seem a little over the top. But in our research into what makes for a consistently high-performing workforce, we've found good reason to care: Happy employees produce more than unhappy ones over the long term. They routinely show up at work, they're less likely to quit, they go above and beyond the call of duty, and they attract people who are just as committed to the job. Moreover, they're not sprinters; they're more like marathon runners, in it for the long haul.

So what does it mean to be happy in your job? It's not about *contentment*, which connotes a degree of complacency. When we and our research partners at the Ross School of Business's Center for Positive Organizational Scholarship started looking into the factors involved in sustainable individual and organizational performance, we found a better word: *thriving*. We think of a thriving workforce as one in which employees are not just satisfied and productive but also engaged in creating the future—the company's and their own. Thriving employees have a bit of an edge: They are highly energized—but they know how to avoid burnout.

Across industries and job types, we found that people who fit our description of thriving demonstrated 16% better overall performance (as reported by their managers) and 125% less burnout (self-reported) than their peers. They were 32% more committed to the organization and 46% more satisfied with their jobs. They also missed much less work and reported significantly fewer doctor visits, which meant health care savings and less lost time for the company.

We've identified two components of thriving. The first is *vitality*: the sense of being alive, passionate, and excited. Employees who experience vitality spark energy in themselves and others. Companies generate vitality by giving people the sense that what they do on a daily basis makes a difference.

The second component is *learning*: the growth that comes from gaining new knowledge and skills. Learning can bestow a technical advantage and status as an expert. Learning can also set in motion a virtuous cycle: People who are developing their abilities are likely to believe in their potential for further growth.

The two qualities work in concert; one without the other is unlikely to be sustainable and may even damage performance. Learning, for instance, creates momentum for a time, but without passion it can lead to burnout. What will I do with what I've learned? Why should I stick with this job? Vitality alone—even when you love the kudos you get for delivering results—can be deadening: When the work doesn't give you opportunities to learn, it's just the same thing over and over again.

The combination of vitality and learning leads to employees who deliver results and find ways to grow. Their work is rewarding not just because they successfully perform what's expected of them today but also because they have a sense of where they and the company are headed. In short, they are thriving, and the energy they create is contagious. (See the sidebar "About the Research.")

How organizations can help employees thrive

Some employees thrive no matter the context. They naturally build vitality and learning into their jobs, and they inspire the people around them. A smart

ABOUT THE RESEARCH

Over the past seven years, we have been researching the nature of thriving in the workplace and the factors that enhance or inhibit it.

Across several studies with our colleagues Cristina Gibson and Flannery Garnett, we surveyed or interviewed more than 1,200 white- and blue-collar employees in an array of industries, including higher education, health care, financial services, maritime, energy, and manufacturing. We also studied metrics reflecting energy, learning, and growth, based on information supplied by employees and bosses, along with retention rates, health, overall job performance, and organizational citizenship behaviors.

We developed a definition of thriving that breaks the concept into two factors: *vitality*—the sense that

(Continued)

you're energized and alive; and *learning*—the gaining of knowledge and skills.

When you put the two together, the statistics are striking. For example, people who were high energy and high learning were 21% more effective as leaders than those who were only high energy. The outcomes on one measure in particular—health—were even more extreme. Those who were high energy and low learning were 54% worse when it came to health than those who were high in both.

hiring manager will look for those people. But most employees are influenced by their environment. Even those predisposed to flourish can fold under pressure.

The good news is that—without heroic measures or major financial investments—leaders and managers can jump-start a culture that encourages employees to thrive. That is, managers can overcome organizational inertia to promote thriving and the productivity that follows it—in many cases with a relatively modest shift in attention.

Ideally, you'd be blessed with a workforce full of people who naturally thrive. But there's a lot you can do to release and sustain enthusiasm. Our research has uncovered four mechanisms that create the conditions for thriving employees: providing decision-making discretion, sharing information, minimizing incivility, and offering performance feedback. The mechanisms overlap somewhat. For instance, if you let people make decisions but give them incomplete information, or leave them exposed to hostile reactions, they'll suffer rather than thrive. One mechanism by itself will get you part of the way, but all four are necessary to create a culture of thriving. Let's look at each in turn.

Providing decision-making discretion

Employees at every level are energized by the ability to make decisions that affect their work. Empowering them in this way gives them a greater sense of control, more say in how things get done, and more opportunities for learning.

The airline industry might seem like an unlikely place to find decision-making discretion (let alone a thriving workforce), but consider one company we studied, Alaska Airlines, which created a culture of empowerment that has contributed to a major turnaround over the past decade. In the early 2000s the airline's numbers were flagging, so senior management launched the 2010 Plan, which explicitly invited employee input into decisions that would improve service while maintaining a reputation for timely departures. Employees were asked to set aside their current perceptions of "good" service and consider new ways to contribute, coming up with ideas that could take service from good to truly great. Agents embraced the program, which gave them, for instance, the discretion to find solutions for customers who had missed flights or were left behind for any other reason. Ron Calvin, the director of the eastern region, told us of a call he had recently received on his cell phone from a customer he hadn't seen or spoken to since working at the Seattle airport, five years earlier. The customer had a three-month-old grandchild who had just gone into cardiac arrest. The grandparents were trying to get back to Seattle from Honolulu. Everything was booked. Ron made a few calls and got them on a flight right away. That day the grandfather sent Ron a text saying, simply, "We made it."

Efforts like this to meet individual needs without holding up flights have led to a number one rating for on-time performance and a full trophy case. The airline has also expanded considerably into new markets, including Hawaii, the Midwest, and the East Coast.

Southwest is a better-known story, largely because of the company's reputation for having a fun and caring culture. Flight attendants are often eager to sing, joke around, and in general entertain customers. They also radiate energy and a passion for learning. One decided to offer the preflight safety instructions in rap format. He was motivated to put his special talents to work, and the passengers loved it, reporting that it was the first time they had actually paid attention to the instructions.

At Facebook, decision-making discretion is fundamental to the culture. One employee posted a note on the site expressing his surprise, and pleasure, at the company's motto, "Move fast and break things," which encourages employees to make decisions and act. On just his second day of work, he found a fix to a complicated bug. He expected some sort of hierarchical review, but his boss, the vice president of product, just smiled and said, "Ship it." He marveled that so early on he had delivered a solution that would instantly reach millions of people.

The challenge for managers is to avoid cutting back on empowerment when people make mistakes. Those situations create the best conditions for learning—not only for the parties concerned but also for others, who can learn vicariously.

Sharing information

Doing your job in an information vacuum is tedious and uninspiring; there's no reason to look for innovative solutions if you can't see the larger impact. People can contribute more effectively when they understand how their work fits with the organization's mission and strategy.

Alaska Airlines has chosen to invest management time in helping employees gain a broad view of the company's strategy. The 2010 Plan was launched with traditional communications but also with a months-long road show and training classes designed to help employees share ideas. The CEO, the president, and the COO still go on the road quarterly to gather information about the idiosyncrasies of various markets; they then disseminate what they've learned. The benefits show up in yearly measures of employee pride in the company—now knocking it out of the park at 90%.

At Zingerman's (an Ann Arbor, Michigan, community of food-related businesses that has worked closely with Wayne Baker, a colleague of ours at the Center for Positive Organizational Scholarship), information is as transparent as possible. The organization had never consciously withheld its numbers—financial information was tacked up for employees to see—but when cofounders Ari Weinzweig and Paul Saginaw studied open book management in the mid-

1990s, they came to believe that employees would show more interest if they got involved in the "game."

Implementation of a more formal and meaningful open book policy was not easy. People could look at the numbers, but they had little reason to pay attention and didn't get much insight into how the data related to their daily work. For the first five or six years, the company struggled to build the concept into its systems and routines and to wrap people's minds around what Baker calls "the rigor of the huddle": weekly gatherings around a whiteboard at which teams track results, "keep score," and forecast the next week's numbers. Although people understood the rules of open book management, at first they didn't see the point of adding yet another meeting to their busy schedules. It wasn't until senior leaders made huddling non-negotiable that employees grasped the true purpose of the whiteboards, which displayed not just financial figures but also service and food quality measures, check averages, internal satisfaction figures, and "fun," which could mean anything from weekly contests to customer satisfaction ratings to employees' ideas for innovation.

Some Zingerman's businesses began instituting "mini games": short-term incentives to find a problem or capitalize on an opportunity. For instance, the staff at Zingerman's Roadhouse restaurant used the greeter game to track how long it took for customers to be greeted. "Ungreeted" customers expressed less satisfaction, and employees found themselves frequently comping purchases to make up for service lapses. The greeter game challenged the host team to greet every customer within five minutes of being seated, with a modest financial reward for 50 straight days of success. It inspired hosts to quickly uncover and fill holes in the service process. Service scores improved considerably over the course of a month. Other Zingerman's businesses started similar games, with incentives for faster delivery, fewer knife injuries in the bakery (which would lower insurance costs), and neater kitchens.

The games have naturally created some internal tensions by delivering the bad news along with the good, which can be demoralizing. But overall they have greatly increased frontline employees' sense of ownership, contributing to better performance. From 2000 to 2010 Zingerman's revenue grew by almost 300%, to more than $35 million. The company's leaders credit open book management as a key factor in that success.

Simple anecdotes lend credence to their claim. For instance, a couple of years ago we saw Ari Weinzweig give a talk at the Roadhouse. A guest asked him whether it was realistic to expect the average waiter or busboy to understand company strategy and finance. In response, Ari turned to a busboy, who had been oblivious to the conversation: Would the teenager mind sharing Zingerman's vision and indicating how well the restaurant was meeting its weekly goals?

Without batting an eye, the busboy stated the vision in his own words and then described how well the restaurant was doing that week on "meals sent back to the kitchen."

While Zingerman's is a fairly small business, much larger ones—such as Whole Foods and the transportation company YRC Worldwide—have also adopted open book management. Systems that make information widely available build trust and give employees the knowledge they need to make good decisions and take initiative with confidence.

Minimizing incivility

The costs of incivility are great. In our research with Christine Pearson, a professor at Arizona State University's Thunderbird School of Global Management, we discovered that half of employees who had experienced uncivil behavior at work intentionally decreased their efforts. More than a third deliberately decreased the quality of their work. Two-thirds spent a lot of time avoiding the offender, and about the same number said their performance had declined.

Most people have experienced rude behavior at work. Here are a few quotes from our research:

> "My boss asked me to prepare an analysis. This was my first project, and I was not given any instructions or examples. He told me the assignment was crap."

> "My boss said, 'If I wanted to know what you thought, I'd ask you.'"

> "My boss saw me remove a paper clip from some documents and drop it in my waste-basket. In front of my 12 subordinates he rebuked me for being wasteful and required me to retrieve it."

"On speakerphone, in front of peers, my boss told me that I'd done 'kindergarten work.'"

We have heard hundreds of stories, and they're sadly familiar to most working people. But we don't hear so much about the costs.

Incivility prevents people from thriving. Those who have been the targets of bad behavior are often, in turn, uncivil themselves: They sabotage their peers. They "forget" to copy colleagues on memos. They spread gossip to deflect attention. Faced with incivility, employees are likely to narrow their focus to avoid risks—and lose opportunities to learn in the process.

A management consultancy we studied, Caiman Consulting, was founded as an alternative to the larger firms. Headquartered in Redmond, Washington, in offices that are not particularly sleek, the firm is recognized for its civil culture. Background checks in its hiring process include a candidate's record of civility.

"People leave a trail," says Caiman's director, Greg Long. "You can save yourself from a corrosive culture by being careful and conscientious up front." The managing director, Raazi Imam, told us, "I have no tolerance for anyone to berate or disrespect someone." When it does happen, he pulls the offender aside to make his policy clear. Long attributes the firm's 95% retention rate to its culture.

Caiman passes up highly qualified candidates who don't match that culture. It also keeps a list of consultants who might be good hires when an appropriate spot opens up. The HR director, Meg Clara, puts strong interpersonal skills and emotional intelligence among her prime criteria for candidates.

At Caiman, as at all companies, managers establish the tone when it comes to civility. A single bad player can set the culture awry. One young manager told us about her boss, an executive who had a habit of yelling from his office "You made a mistake!" for a sin as minor as a typo. His voice would resonate across the floor, making everyone cringe and the recipient feel acutely embarrassed. Afterward, colleagues would gather in a common area for coffee and commiseration. An insider told us that those conversations focused not on how to get ahead at the company or learn to cope by developing a thick skin but on how to get even and get out.

In our research, we were surprised by how few companies consider civility—or incivility—when evaluating candidates. Corporate culture is inherently contagious; employees assimilate to their environment. In other words, if you hire for civility, you're more likely to breed it into your culture. (See the sidebar "Individual Strategies for Thriving.")

Offering performance feedback

Feedback creates opportunities for learning and the energy that's so critical for a culture of thriving. By resolving feelings of uncertainty, feedback keeps

INDIVIDUAL STRATEGIES FOR THRIVING

Although organizations benefit from enabling employees to thrive, leaders have so much on their plates that attention to this important task can slip. However, anyone can adopt strategies to enhance learning and vitality without significant organizational support. And because thriving can be contagious, you may find your ideas quickly spreading.

Take a break

Research by Jim Loehr and Tony Schwartz has shown that breaks and other renewal tactics, no matter how small, can create positive energy.

In our teaching, we let students design regular breaks and activities into the class to ensure that they stay energized. In one term, students decided to halt every class for two minutes at the midpoint to get up and do something active. Each week a different

(Continued)

foursome designed the quick activity—watching a funny YouTube video, doing the cha-cha slide, or playing a game. The point is that the students figure out what is energizing for them and share it with the class.

Even if your organization doesn't offer formal mechanisms for renewal, it's nearly always possible to schedule a short walk, a bike ride, or a quick lunch in the park. Some people write it into their schedules so that meetings can't impinge.

Craft your own work to be more meaningful

You can't ignore the requirements of your job, but you can watch for opportunities to make it more meaningful. Consider Tina, the staff administrator of a policy think tank within a large organization. When her boss took a six-month sabbatical, Tina needed to find a short-term replacement project. After some

scouting, she uncovered a budding initiative to develop staff members' ability to speak up with their
ideas about the organization. The effort needed an
innovative spirit to kick it off. The pay was lower, but
the nature of the work energized Tina. When her boss
returned, she renegotiated the terms of her think
tank job to consume only 80% of her time, leaving the
rest for the staff development project.

Look for opportunities to innovate and learn

Breaking out of the status quo can trigger the learning that is so essential to thriving. When Roger became the head of a prestigious high school in the
Midwest, he was brimming with innovative ideas. He
quickly ascertained, however, that quite a few staff
members were not open to new ways of doing things.

(Continued)

123

He made sure to listen to their concerns and tried to bring them along, but he invested more of his effort in the growth and learning of those who shared his passion for breakthrough ideas. Mentoring and encouraging them, Roger began to achieve small wins, and his initiatives gained some momentum. A few of the resisters ended up leaving the school, and others came around when they saw signs of positive change. By focusing on those bright spots rather than the points of resistance, Roger was able to launch an effort that is propelling the school toward a radically different future.

Invest in relationships that energize you

All of us have colleagues who may be brilliant but are difficult and corrosive to work with. Individuals who thrive look for opportunities to work closely with colleagues who generate energy and to minimize interaction with those who deplete it. In fact, when we built the research team to study thriving, we chose colleagues we enjoyed, who energized us, with whom we looked forward to spending time, and from whom we knew we could learn. We seek to build good relationships by starting every meeting with good news or expressions of gratitude.

Recognize that thriving can spill over outside the office

There's evidence that high levels of engagement at work will not lessen your ability to thrive in your personal life but instead can enhance it. When one of us (Gretchen) was dealing with her husband's difficult medical diagnosis, she found that her work,

(Continued)

125

even though it was demanding, gave her the energy to thrive professionally and in her family life. Thriving is not a zero-sum game. People who feel energized at work often bring that energy to their lives beyond work. And people inspired by outside activities—volunteering, training for a race, taking a class—can bring their drive back to the office.

people's work-related activities focused on personal and organizational goals. The quicker and more direct the feedback, the more useful it is.

The Zingerman's huddle, described earlier, is a tool for sharing near-real-time information about individual as well as business performance. Leaders outline daily ups and downs on the whiteboard, and employees are expected to "own" the numbers and come up with ideas for getting back on track when necessary. The huddles also include "code reds" and "code greens," which document customer complaints and compliments so that all employees can learn and grow on the basis of immediate and tangible feedback.

Quicken Loans, a mortgage finance company that measures and rewards employee performance like no other organization, offers continually updated performance feedback using two types of dashboards: a ticker and kanban reports. (*Kanban*, a Japanese word meaning "signal," is used frequently in operations.)

The ticker has several panels that display group and individual metrics along with data feeds that show how likely an employee is to meet his or her daily goals. People are hardwired to respond to scores and goals, so the metrics help keep them energized through the day; essentially, they're competing against their own numbers.

The kanban dashboard allows managers to track people's performance so that they know when an employee or a team needs some coaching or other type of assistance. A version of the kanban chart is also displayed on monitors, with a rotating list of the top 15 salespeople for each metric. Employees are constantly in competition to make the boards, which are almost like a video game's ranking of high scorers.

Employees could feel overwhelmed or even oppressed by the constant nature of the feedback. Instead, the company's strong norms for civility and respect and for giving employees a say in how they accomplish their work create a context in which the feedback is energizing and promotes growth.

The global law firm O'Melveny & Myers lauds the use of 360-degree evaluations in helping workers thrive. The feedback is open-ended and summarized rather than shared verbatim, which has encouraged a 97% response rate. Carla Christofferson, the managing partner of the Los Angeles offices, learned from her evaluation that people saw her behavior as not matching the firm's stated commitment to work-life balance—which was causing stress among employees. She started to spend more time away from the office and to limit weekend work to things she could do at home. She became a role model for balance, which went a long way toward eliminating the worry of employees who wanted a life outside of work.

The four mechanisms that help employees thrive don't require enormous efforts or investments. What they do require is leaders who are open to empowering employees and who set the tone. As we've noted, each mechanism provides a different angle that's necessary for thriving. You can't choose one or two from the menu; the mechanisms reinforce one another. For example, can people be comfortable making decisions if they don't have honest information about current numbers? Can they make effective decisions if they're worried about being ridiculed?

Creating the conditions for thriving requires your concerted attention. Helping people grow and remain energized at work is valiant on its own merits—but it can also boost your company's performance in a sustainable way.

GRETCHEN SPREITZER is the Keith E. and Valerie J. Alessi Professor of Business Administration at the University of Michigan's Ross School of Business where she is a core faculty member in the Center for Positive Organizations. CHRISTINE PORATH is an associate professor of management at Georgetown University, the author of *Mastering Civility: A Manifesto for the Workplace* (Grand Central Publishing, 2016), and a coauthor of *The Cost of Bad Behavior* (Portfolio, 2009).

Reprinted from *Harvard Business Review*, January–February 2012 (product #R1201F).

6

The Research We've Ignored About Happiness at Work

By André Spicer and Carl Cederström

Recently, we found ourselves in motivational seminars at our respective places of employment. Both events preached the gospel of happiness. In one, a speaker explained that happiness could make you healthier, kinder, more productive, and even more likely to get promoted.

The other seminar involved mandatory dancing of the wilder kind. It was supposed to fill our bodies with joy. It also prompted one of us to sneak out and take refuge in the nearest bathroom.

Ever since a group of scientists switched the lights on and off at the Hawthorne factory in the mid-1920s, scholars and executives alike have been obsessed with increasing their employees' productivity. In particular, happiness as a way to boost productivity seems to have gained traction in corporate circles as of late.[1] Firms spend money on happiness coaches, team-building exercises, gameplays, funsultants, and chief happiness officers (yes, you'll find one of those at Google). These activities and titles may appear jovial or even bizarre, but companies are taking them extremely seriously. Should they?

When you look closely at the research—which we did after the dancing incident—it's not clear that encouraging happiness at work is always a good idea. Sure, there is evidence to suggest that happy employees are less likely to leave, more likely to satisfy customers, are safer, and more likely to engage in citizenship behavior.[2] However, we also discovered alternate findings, which indicates that some of the taken-for-granted wisdoms about what happiness can achieve in the workplace are mere myths.

To start, we don't really know what happiness is or how to measure it. Measuring happiness is about as easy as taking the temperature of the soul or determining the exact color of love. As historian Darrin M. McMahon shows in his illuminating book *Happiness: A History*, ever since the sixth century BC, when Croesus is said to have quipped "No one who lives is happy," this slippery concept has served as a proxy for all sorts of other concepts, from pleasure and joy to plenitude and contentment. Being happy in the moment, Samuel Johnson said, could be achieved only when drunk.[3] For Jean-Jacques Rousseau, happiness was to lie in a boat, drifting aimlessly, feeling like a God (not exactly the picture of productivity). There are other definitions of happiness, too, but they are neither less nor more plausible than those of Johnson or Rousseau.

And just because we have more-advanced technology today doesn't mean we're any closer to pinning down a definition, as Will Davies reminds us in his book *The Happiness Industry.* He concludes that even as we have developed more-advanced techniques for measuring emotions and predicting behaviors, we have also adopted increasingly simplified notions of what it means to be human, let alone what it means to pursue happiness. A brain scan that lights up may *seem* like it's telling us something concrete about an elusive emotion, for example, when it actually isn't.

Happiness doesn't necessarily lead to increased productivity. A stream of research shows some contradictory results about the relationship between happiness—which is often defined as "job satisfaction"—and productivity.[4] One study on British supermarkets even suggests there might be a negative correlation between job satisfaction and corporate productivity: The more miserable the employees were, the better the profits.[5] Sure, other studies have pointed in the opposite direction, saying that there is a link between feeling content with work and being productive. But even these studies, when considered as a whole, demonstrate a relatively weak correlation.

Happiness can also be exhausting. The pursuit of happiness may not be wholly effective, but it doesn't really hurt, right? Wrong. Ever since the eighteenth century, people have been pointing out that the demand to be happy brings with it a heavy burden, a responsibility that can never be perfectly fulfilled. Focusing on happiness can actually make us feel less happy.

A psychological experiment recently demonstrated this.[6] The researchers asked their subjects to watch a film that would usually make them happy: a figure skater winning a medal. But before watching the film, half of the group was asked to read a statement aloud about the importance of happiness in life. The other half did not read the statement. The researchers were surprised to find that those who had read the statement were actually *less* happy after watching the film. Essentially, when happiness becomes a duty, it can make people feel worse if they fail to accomplish it.

This is particularly problematic at the present era, in which happiness is preached as a moral obligation.[7] As the French philosopher Pascal Bruckner put it, "Unhappiness is not only unhappiness; it is, worse yet, a failure to be happy."[8]

Happiness won't necessarily get you through the workday. If you've worked in a frontline customer service job, like a call center or a fast food restaurant, you know that being upbeat is not optional—it's compulsory. And as tiring as that may be, it makes some sense when you're in front of customers.

But today, many non-customer-facing employees are also asked to be upbeat. This could have some unforeseen consequences. One study found that people who were in a good mood were worse at picking out acts of deception than those who were in a bad mood.[9] Another piece of research found that people who were angry during a negotiation achieved better outcomes than people who were happy.[10] This suggests that being happy may not be good for all aspects of our work or for jobs that rely heavily on certain abilities. In fact, in some cases, happiness can actually make our performance worse.

Happiness could damage your relationship with your boss. If we believe that work is where we will find happiness, we might, in some cases, start to mistake our boss for a surrogate spouse or parent. In her study of a media company, researcher Susanne Ekmann found that those who expected work to make them happy would often become emotionally needy.[11] They wanted their managers to provide them with a steady stream of recognition and emotional reassurance. And when they *didn't* receive the expected emotional response (which was often), these employees felt neglected and started overreacting. Even minor setbacks were interpreted as being rejected by their bosses. So in many ways, expecting a boss to bring happiness makes us emotionally vulnerable.

Happiness could also hurt your relationships with friends and family. In her book *Cold Intimacies*, sociology professor Eva Illouz points out a strange side effect of people trying to live more emotionally at work: They started to treat their private lives like work tasks. The people she spoke with saw their personal lives as something that needed to be carefully administered using a range of tools and techniques they had learned from corporate life. As a result, their home lives became increasingly cold and calculating. It's no wonder then that many of the people she spoke with preferred to spend time at work rather than at home.

Happiness could make losing your job that much more devastating. When we expect the workplace to provide happiness and meaning in our lives, we become dangerously dependent on it. When studying professionals, sociology professor Richard Sennett noticed that people who saw their employer as an important source of personal meaning were those who became most devastated if they were fired.[12] When these people lost their jobs, they weren't just losing an income—they were losing the promise of happiness. This suggests that, when we see our work as a great source of happiness, we make ourselves emotionally vulnerable during periods of change. In an era of constant corporate restructuring, this can be dangerous.

Happiness could also make you selfish. Being happy makes you a better person, right? Not so, according to an interesting piece of research.[13] Participants were given lottery tickets and then given a choice about how many tickets they wanted to give to others and how many they wished to keep for themselves. Those who were in a good mood ended up keeping more tickets for themselves. This implies that, at least in some settings, being happy doesn't necessarily mean we will be generous. In fact, the opposite could be true.

Finally, happiness could also make you lonely. In one experiment, psychologists asked a number of people to keep a detailed diary for two weeks. What they found at the end of the study was that those who greatly valued happiness felt lonelier than those who valued happiness less.[14] It seems that focusing too much on the pursuit of happiness can make us feel disconnected from other people.

So why, contrary to all of this evidence, do we continue to hold on to the belief that happiness can improve a workplace? The answer, according to one study, comes down to aesthetics and ideology. Happiness is a convenient idea that looks good on paper (the aesthetic part). But it's also an idea that helps us shy away from more serious issues at work, such as conflicts and workplace politics (the ideological part).[15]

When we assume that happy workers are better workers, we may sweep more uncomfortable questions under the rug, especially since happiness is often seen as a choice. It becomes a convenient way of dealing with negative attitudes, party poopers, miserable bastards, and other unwanted characters in corporate life. Invoking happiness, in all its ambiguity, is an excellent way of getting away with controversial decisions, such as choosing to let people go. As Barbara Ehrenreich points out in her book *Bright-Sided*, positive messages about happiness have proved particularly popular in times of crisis and mass layoffs.

Given all these potential problems, we think there is a strong case for rethinking our expectation that work should always make us happy. It can be exhausting, make us overreact, drain our personal life of meaning, increase our vulnerability, and make us more gullible, selfish, and lonely. Most striking is that consciously pursuing happiness can actually drain the sense of joy we usually get from the really good things we experience.

In reality, work—like all other aspects of life—is likely to make us feel a wide range of emotions. If your job feels depressing and meaningless, it might be because it *is* depressing and meaningless. Pretending otherwise can just make it worse. Happiness, of course, is a great thing to experience, but it can't be willed into existence. Maybe the less we seek to actively pursue happiness through our jobs, the more likely we will be to actually experience a sense of joy in our work—a joy that is spontaneous and pleasurable rather than constructed and oppressive. But most important, we will be better equipped to cope with work in a sober manner. To see it for what it is and not what we—whether as executives, employees, or dancing motivational seminar leaders—pretend that it is.

ANDRÉ SPICER is a professor of organizational behavior at Cass Business School in London. CARL CEDERSTRÖM is an associate professor of organization theory at Stockholm University. They are the coauthors of *The Wellness Syndrome* (Polity 2015).

Notes

1. C. D. Fisher, "Happiness at Work." *International Journal of Management Reviews* 12, no. 4 (December 2010): 384–412.
2. Ibid.
3. D. M. McMahon, *Happiness: A History.* (New York: Atlantic Monthly Press, 2006.)
4. Fisher, "Happiness at Work."
5. McMahon, *Happiness: A History.*
6. I. B. Mauss et al., "Can Seeking Happiness Make People Happy? Paradoxical Effects of Valuing Happiness." *Emotion* 11, no. 4 (August 2011): 807–815.
7. P. Bruckner, *Perpetual Euphoria: On the Duty to Be Happy*, tr. Steven Rendall. (Princeton, New Jersey: Princeton University Press, 2011.)
8. Ibid, 5.
9. J. P. Forgas and R. East, "On Being Happy and Gullible: Mood Effects on Skepticism and the Detection of Deception." *Journal of Experimental Social Psychology* 44 (2008): 1362–1367.

10. G. A. van Kleef et al., "The Interpersonal Effects of Anger and Happiness in Negotiations." *Journal of Personality and Social Psychology* 86, no. 1 (2004): 57–76.

11. S. Ekman, "Fantasies About Work as Limitless Potential—How Managers and Employees Seduce Each Other through Dynamics of Mutual Recognition." *Human Relations* 66, no. 9 (December 2012): 1159–1181.

12. R. Sennett, *The Corrosion of Character: The Personal Consequences of Work in New Capitalism.* (New York: W.W. Norton, 2000.)

13. H. B. Tan and J. Forgas, "When Happiness Makes Us Selfish, But Sadness Makes Us Fair: Affective Influences on Interpersonal Strategies in the Dictator Game." *Journal of Experimental Social Psychology* 46, no. 3 (May 2010): 571–576.

14. I. B. Mauss, "The Pursuit of Happiness Can Be Lonely." *Emotion* 12, no. 5 (2012): 908–912.

15. G. E. Ledford, "Happiness and Productivity Revisited." *Journal of Organizational Behavior* 20, no. 1 (January 1999): 25–30.

Adapted from content posted on hbr.org on
July 21, 2015 (product #H027TW).

7

The Happiness Backlash

By Alison Beard

Nothing depresses me more than reading about happiness. Why? Because there's entirely too much advice out there about how to achieve it. As Frédéric Lenoir points out in *Happiness: A Philosopher's Guide* (recently translated from its original French), great thinkers have been discussing this topic for more than 2,000 years. But opinions on it still differ. Just scan the 14,700 titles listed in the "happiness" subgenre of self-help books on Amazon, or watch the 55 TED talks tagged in the same category. What makes us happy? Health, money, social connection, purpose, "flow," generosity, gratitude, inner peace, positive thinking . . . research shows that any (or all?) of the above answers are correct. Social scientists tell us that even the simplest of tricks—counting our blessings, meditating for 10 minutes a day, forcing smiles—can push us into a happier state of mind.

And yet for me and many others, happiness remains elusive. Of course, I sometimes feel joyful and content—reading a bedtime story to my kids, interviewing someone I greatly admire, finishing a tough piece of writing. But despite having good health, supportive family and friends, and a stimulating and flexible job, I'm often awash in negative emotions: worry, frustration, anger, disappointment, guilt, envy, regret. My default state is dissatisfied.

The huge and growing body of happiness literature promises to lift me out of these feelings. But the effect is more like kicking me when I'm down. I know I should be happy. I know I have every reason to be and that I'm better off than most. I know that happier people are more successful. I know that just a few mental exercises might help me. Still, when I'm in a bad mood, it's hard to break out of it. And—I'll admit—a small part of me regards my nonbliss not as unproductive negativity but as highly productive realism. I can't imagine being happy all the time; indeed, I'm highly suspicious of anyone who claims to be.

I agreed to write this essay because over the past several years I've sensed a swell of support for this point of view. Barbara Ehrenreich's 2009 book *Bright-Sided*, about the "relentless promotion" and undermining effects of positive thinking, was followed last year by *Rethinking Positive Thinking*, by the NYU psychology professor Gabriele Oettingen, and *The Upside of Your Dark Side*, by two experts in positive psychology, Todd Kashdan and Robert Biswas-Diener. This year brought a terrific *Psychology Today* article by Matthew Hutson titled "Beyond Happiness: The Upside of Feeling Down"; *The Upside of Stress*, by Stanford's Kelly McGonigal; *Beyond Happiness*, by the British historian and commentator Anthony Seldon; and *The Happiness Industry:*

How the Government and Big Business Sold Us Well-Being, by another Brit, the Goldsmiths lecturer in politics William Davies.

Are we finally seeing a backlash against happiness? Sort of. Most of these recent releases rail against our modern obsession with *feeling* happy and *thinking* positively. Oettingen explains the importance of damping sunny fantasies with sober analysis of the obstacles in one's way. Kashdan and Biswas-Diener's book and Hutson's article detail the benefits we derive from all the negative emotions I cited earlier; taken together, those feelings spur us to better our circumstances and ourselves. (The Harvard psychologist Susan David, a coauthor of the HBR article "Emotional Agility," also writes thoughtfully on this topic.)

McGonigal shows how viewing one unhappy condition—stress—in a kinder light can turn it into something that improves rather than hurts our health. Those who accept feeling stressed as the body's natural response to a challenge are more resilient and live longer than those who try to fight it.

Seldon describes his own progression from pleasure seeking to more-meaningful endeavors that bring him (and should bring us) joy. Sadly, he trivializes his advice by alphabetizing it: Accepting oneself; Belonging to a group; having good Character, Discipline, Empathy, Focus, Generosity, and Health; using Inquiry; embarking on an inner Journey; accepting Karma; and embracing both Liturgy and Meditation. (One wonders what he'll use for X and Z in the next book.)

Davies comes at the issue from a different angle. He's fed up with organizational attempts to tap into what is essentially a "grey mushy process inside our brains." In his view, there's something sinister about the way advertisers, HR managers, governments, and pharmaceutical companies are measuring, manipulating, and ultimately making money from our insatiable desire to be happier.

But none of these authors is arguing against individuals' aspiring to have a generally happy life. We call that the pursuit of "happiness," but what we really mean is "long-term fulfillment." Martin Seligman, the father of positive psychology, calls it "flourishing" and said years ago that positive emotion (that is, feeling happy) is only one element of it, along with engagement, relationships, meaning, and achievement. In the parlance Arianna Huffington uses in her recent book, it's "thriving," and Lenoir, whose history of happiness philosophy is probably the most enlightening and entertaining of the bunch, describes it as simply "love of life." Who can argue against any of those things?

Where most of the happiness gurus go wrong is insisting that daily if not constant happiness is a means to long-term fulfillment. For some glass-half-full optimists, that may be true. They can "stumble on happiness" the way the field's most prominent researcher, Dan Gilbert, suggests; or gain "the happiness advantage" that the professor-turned-consultant Shawn Achor talks about; or "broadcast happiness," as Michelle Gielan, Achor's wife and partner at the firm GoodThink, recommends in her new book. As I said, it apparently takes just a few simple tricks.

But for the rest of us, that much cheer feels forced, so it's unlikely to help us mold meaningful relationships or craft the perfect career. It certainly can't be drawn out of us by employers or other external forces. We pursue fulfillment in different ways, without reading self-help books. And I suspect that in the long run we'll be OK—perhaps even happy.

ALISON BEARD is a senior editor at *Harvard Business Review*.

Reprinted from *Harvard Business Review*,
July–August 2015.

Index

Invaluable insights
always at your fingertips

With an All-Access subscription to
Harvard Business Review, you'll get
so much more than a magazine.

Exclusive online content and tools
you can put to use today

My Library, your personal workspace for sharing,
saving, and organizing HBR.org articles and tools

Unlimited access to more than 4,000 articles in the
Harvard Business Review archive

Subscribe today at hbr.org/subnow

The most important management ideas all in one place.

We hope you enjoyed this book from *Harvard Business Review*. For the best ideas HBR has to offer turn to HBR's 10 Must Reads Boxed Set. From books on leadership and strategy to managing yourself and others, this 6-book collection delivers articles on the most essential business topics to help you succeed.

HBR's 10 Must Reads Series

The definitive collection of ideas and best practices on our most sought-after topics from the best minds in business.

- Change Management
- Collaboration
- Communication
- Emotional Intelligence
- Innovation
- Leadership
- Making Smart Decisions

- Managing Across Cultures
- Managing People
- Managing Yourself
- Strategic Marketing
- Strategy
- Teams
- The Essentials

hbr.org/mustreads

Buy for your team, clients, or event.
Visit hbr.org/bulksales for quantity discount rates.